Gooseberry patch

Our Favorite
Soup & Sandwich

Copyright 2024, Gooseberry Patch

Here's a handy way to easily pour two flavors of chilled soup into a bowl at the same time. Fill two small cream pitchers with each flavor of soup, then pour. The pitchers' small size makes pouring so easy!

Chilled Melon Soup

3 c. cantaloupe melon, peeled,
  seeded and chopped
2 T. sugar, divided
1/4 c. orange juice, divided
1/8 t. salt, divided

3 c. honeydew melon, peeled,
  seeded and chopped
Garnish: fresh mint sprigs or
  orange slices

In a blender, process cantaloupe, half the sugar, half the juice and half the salt until smooth. Cover and refrigerate. Repeat with honeydew and remaining ingredients except garnish. Refrigerate, covered, in separate containers. To serve, pour equal amounts of each mixture at the same time on opposite sides of individual soup bowls. Garnish as desired.

Need to add a little zing to a pot of soup?
Just add a dash of balsamic or
herb-flavored vinegar.

Cold Zucchini Soup

4 zucchini, quartered and sliced
1 bunch green onions, chopped
4 c. chicken broth
1 t. salt
1 t. pepper

2 8-oz pkgs. cream cheese, cubed and softened
1 t. fresh dill, snipped
8-oz. container sour cream
Optional: chopped fresh chives

In a saucepan over medium-high heat, combine zucchini, onions, broth, salt and pepper. Cook, stirring occasionally, for 20 minutes. Stir in cream cheese and dill. Process soup in batches in a blender until smooth. Stir in sour cream. Cover and chill for 8 hours. Garnish with chives, if desired.

A simple bouquet that's perfect for a casual supper of soup and cornbread! Pick up a bunch of dewy-fresh cut flowers at the local market and tuck them into a canning jar.

Chilled Beet Soup

Serves 2

1-1/2 c. warm water
15-oz. can whole red beets,
    drained and juice reserved
1 cucumber, chopped

4 green onions, chopped
2 c. sour cream
6 to 7 T. cider vinegar, divided
salt to taste

In a bowl, combine water and reserved beet juice; set aside. Grate beets
and add to bowl along with cucumber, onions, sour cream, 6 tablespoons
vinegar and salt. Use a whisk to mix well. If flavor isn't sour enough,
add one more tablespoon of vinegar. Cover and chill in refrigerator
until cold.

As you walk down the fairway of life you must
smell the roses, for you only get to play one round.

—Ben Hogan

Apple-Chicken Salad Sandwich   *Makes 2 sandwiches*

1 boneless, skinless chicken
    breast, grilled and cubed
2 T. mayonnaise, or to taste
1 T. sunflower kernels
1 T. dried cranberries

1/2 red onion, chopped
1 apple, cored and cubed
salt and pepper to taste
2 sandwich buns, split

Combine all ingredients except buns in a large bowl; stir well. Place buns, split-side up, under a broiler to toast. Fill buns evenly with chicken mixture.

A basket of fresh-baked muffins turns
a bowl of soup into a meal! Serve warm
with lots of butter.

Apple-Raisin Muffins

Makes 6 to 8 muffins

9-oz. pkg. apple-cinnamon
   muffin mix
2 T. milk
1 egg, beaten

1 c. Gala or Golden Delicious
   apple, peeled and grated
1/2 c. raisins

Combine muffin mix, milk and egg in a large bowl; stir until well moistened. Fold in fruit. Spoon batter into greased muffin cups, filling 2/3 full. Bake at 400 degrees for 20 to 25 minutes.

Leeks are delicious, but are often sandy when purchased.
To quickly clean them, slice into 2-inch lengths and soak
in a bowl of cold water. Swish them in the water and drain.
Refill the bowl, and swish again until the water is clear.
Drain, pat dry and they're ready to use.

Cream of Vegetable Soup

Serves 8

3/4 c. butter
3/4 c. onion, diced
1-1/2 c. potatoes, peeled
    and diced
3/4 c. tomato, diced
3/4 c. carrot, peeled and diced
3/4 c. green beans, diced
3/4 c. broccoli, coarsely chopped

3/4 c. leek, minced
3/4 c. zucchini, minced
1 clove garlic, minced
1-1/2 t. sugar, or to taste
salt and pepper to taste
6 c. chicken broth
1/2 c. whipping cream
Garnish: chopped fresh parsley

Melt butter in a large soup pot over medium heat. Add onion and sauté until tender, 5 to 10 minutes. Reduce heat to medium-low; add remaining ingredients except cream and garnish. Cover and cook until vegetables are tender, about 20 to 25 minutes. Bring to a boil. Reduce heat to low; cover and simmer for 10 minutes. Let cool slightly. With an immersion blender, process soup until smooth. Increase heat to medium; gradually stir in cream. Heat through without boiling. Garnish with parsley.

Try substituting canned evaporated milk for
half-and-half or whole milk. It's handy to keep
in the pantry, doesn't need refrigeration and
is lower in fat too.

Easy Cheesy Broccoli Soup

Makes 8 servings

14-oz. pkg. frozen broccoli
    flowerets
2 10-3/4 oz. cans Cheddar
    cheese soup

2 c. milk
1 T. all-purpose flour
2 c. shredded Cheddar cheese,
    divided

Place frozen broccoli in a microwave-safe casserole dish. Microwave on high for 5 minutes. Meanwhile, whisk together soup, milk and flour in a soup pot. Stir until smooth; cook over medium-low heat until warmed through. Drain cooked broccoli; add to soup mixture. Cook for 10 minutes over medium heat, stirring frequently. Add cheese, reserving 1/4 cup for garnish. Cook over low heat for an additional 3 minutes. Ladle into soup bowls and top with a sprinkle of reserved cheese.

Don't blow your top! When blending hot liquids, be sure to
remove the stopper from the top of your blender so steam
pressure doesn't build up inside. After removing the stopper,
cover the hole with a clean, folded kitchen towel to prevent
a mess before blending.

Cream of Cauliflower Soup

1 head cauliflower, chopped
2 c. chicken broth
2 T. reduced-sodium chicken
    bouillon granules
2 c. half-and-half
2 c. milk
1 carrot, peeled and shredded
2 bay leaves

1/4 t. garlic powder
1/2 c. instant mashed potato
    flakes
1 c. shredded Monterey Jack
    cheese
1 c. shredded Cheddar cheese
Garnish: paprika or minced
    fresh parsley

In a large saucepan, combine cauliflower, broth and bouillon. Bring to a
boil. Reduce heat to medium-low; cover and cook for 20 minutes, or
until cauliflower is tender. Mash cauliflower in saucepan. Transfer entire
contents of saucepan to a 3-quart slow cooker. Stir in half-and-half, milk,
carrot, bay leaves and garlic powder. Cover and cook on low setting for
3 hours. Stir in potato flakes; cook 30 minutes longer, or until thickened.
Discard bay leaves. Cool slightly. Using an immersion blender, process
soup until smooth. Stir in cheeses. Cover and cook until soup is heated
through and cheese is melted. Garnish servings with paprika or parsley.

Fill up a relish tray with crunchy fresh cut-up veggies
as a simple side dish for sandwiches. A creamy
salad dressing can even do double duty as
a veggie dip and a sandwich spread.

Turkey Panini

Makes 2 sandwiches

1/4 c. whole-berry cranberry
    sauce
2 to 3 t. prepared horseradish
2 T. mayonnaise
4 large slices ciabatta bread,
    1/2-inch thick
4 slices cooked turkey breast or
    deli turkey, 3/8-inch thick

salt and pepper to taste
4 slices provolone cheese
4 slices bacon, crisply cooked
1-1/2 T. olive oil
Optional: mixed salad greens

Combine cranberry sauce and horseradish; stir well and set aside.
Spread mayonnaise on one side of each slice of bread. Spread cranberry-horseradish sauce on 2 slices of bread; top each sandwich with 2 turkey slices and sprinkle with salt and pepper. Arrange 2 cheese slices on each sandwich; top with 2 bacon slices. Cover with remaining bread slices, mayonnaise-side down. Brush tops and bottoms of sandwiches with olive oil. Cook on a panini press for 3 minutes, or until cheese begins to melt and bread is toasted. Garnish with mixed salad greens, if desired. Serve hot.

In any favorite gazpacho recipe, swap out the tomatoes for avocados, or try unflavored yogurt for a yummy white gazpacho.

Garden-Fresh Gazpacho

Serves 12

8 tomatoes, chopped
1 onion, finely chopped
1 cucumber, peeled and chopped
1 green pepper, chopped
2 T. fresh parsley or cilantro,
    chopped
1 clove garlic, finely chopped

2 stalks celery, chopped
2 T. lemon juice
salt and pepper to taste
4 c. tomato juice
4 drops hot pepper sauce
Optional: sour cream

Combine all ingredients except sour cream, if using, in a large lidded container or gallon-size Mason jar. Refrigerate until well chilled. Dollop servings with sour cream, if desired.

Try something new for brown-bag lunches...roll any combination of cheese, deli meat and veggies in a tortilla. Even a kid-friendly peanut butter & jelly wrap tastes terrific!

Cool Summer Squash Soup

1 clove garlic, minced
1/4 c. olive oil
1 c. sweet onion, chopped
1 to 2 yellow squash, sliced
1 to 2 zucchini, sliced
16-oz. can diced tomatoes

Optional: 1/2 spaghetti squash
14-1/2 oz. can chicken or
   vegetable broth
1/4 t. dried oregano
1/4 t. dried parsley
salt and pepper to taste

In a large saucepan over medium heat, sauté garlic in oil. Remove garlic; add onion and squash. Sauté until soft. To a large soup pot, add squash mixture and remaining ingredients. Simmer for 30 minutes; cool. Refrigerate until ready to serve.

Spaghetti Squash Variation:

Microwave spaghetti squash on high setting, cut-side down, for 8 minutes, or until easy to pierce. Remove seeds; with a fork, scrape out pulp which will resemble spaghetti. Cool; add pulp to soup mixture.

There's no such thing as too much chili! Top hot dogs and baked potatoes with extra chili. You can even spoon chili into flour tortillas and sprinkle with shredded cheese for quick burritos.

Michelle's Spicy Vegetarian Chili

Serves 6 to 8

2 T. olive oil
1 onion, chopped
1-1/2 c. frozen tri-colored
    sliced peppers, chopped
1 T. garlic, minced
1-1/4 oz. pkg. taco seasoning mix
1 t. ground cumin
28-oz. can diced tomatoes

15-oz. can black-eyed peas
15-oz. can black beans
Optional: 15-oz. can garbanzo
    beans
1 c. fresh or frozen corn
11-oz. pkg. fresh baby spinach
2 T. lemon juice
Garnish: sour cream

Heat oil in a large Dutch oven over medium heat. Sauté onion, peppers and garlic in oil until tender, about 6 to 8 minutes. Add taco seasoning and cumin to onion mixture; mix well and cook for an additional minute. Add undrained tomatoes and all undrained beans. Stir to mix; add frozen corn. Simmer for about 10 minutes, until corn is heated through. Remove from heat; fold in spinach and lemon juice. Cover and let stand 5 minutes to wilt spinach. Top individual servings with a dollop of sour cream.

Garden-fresh herbs give a wonderful flavor boost
to foods! If a recipe calls for one teaspoon of
a dried herb, simply substitute one tablespoon of
the chopped fresh herb.

Tuna & Egg Salad Sandwiches

Makes 4 sandwiches

2 6-oz. cans white tuna, drained
    and flaked
1/4 c. celery, minced
2 T. onion, minced
salt and pepper to taste
2 eggs, hard-boiled, peeled
    and halved

1/3 c. mayonnaise
8 slices Italian bread
Garnish: lettuce leaves, tomato
    slices, pickles

In a large bowl, combine tuna, celery, onion, salt and pepper to taste. Chop egg whites and add to mixture, setting aside yolks for another recipe. Mix well and add mayonnaise to desired consistency. Serve on bread, garnished as desired with lettuce, tomatoes and pickles.

Only using part of an onion? The remaining half
will stay fresh for days when rubbed with butter
or oil and stored in the refrigerator.

Tuna Panini

12-oz. can tuna, drained
1/2 c. onion, chopped
2 dill pickle spears, chopped
3/4 c. carrot, peeled, shredded
    and chopped

3/4 c. shredded mozzarella cheese
2 T. mayonnaise
1 T. olive oil
8 slices multi-grain bread, toasted
1 tomato, sliced

In a bowl, mix tuna, onion, pickles, carrot, cheese and mayonnaise. In a panini press or skillet, heat olive oil over medium heat until hot. For each sandwich, top one slice of toasted bread with tuna mixture, 2 slices of tomato and second slice of bread. Place sandwich in panini press or skillet; cook for one to 2 minutes, until cheese is melted.

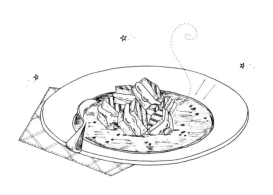

Try something new...grilled cheese croutons!
Make grilled cheese sandwiches as usual, then slice
them into small squares. Toss into a bowl of
creamy tomato soup...yum!

Garlicky Tomato Soup

3 tomatoes, cubed
2 green, red or yellow peppers,
    cut into bite-size pieces
10 cloves garlic, coarsely chopped
    and divided

1/2 c. olive oil
2 c. water
2 t. salt
pepper to taste

Combine tomatoes, peppers and half the garlic in a food processor. Pulse
until tomatoes and peppers are chopped; set aside. Heat oil in a saucepan
over medium heat. Add tomato mixture and cook, stirring often, about
5 minutes. Add remaining ingredients; bring to a boil. Reduce heat to
low and simmer for 10 minutes

Nothing perks up the flavor of tomato soup like fresh basil! Keep a pot of basil in the kitchen windowsill and just pinch off a few leaves whenever they're needed.

Tomato Bisque

Makes 6 servings

2 c. chicken broth
14-1/2 oz. can whole tomatoes,
    broken up
1/2 c. celery, chopped
1/2 c. onion, chopped

3 tomatoes, chopped
3 T. butter
3 T. all-purpose flour
2 c. half-and-half
1 T. sugar

In a large saucepan over medium heat, combine broth, canned tomatoes with juice, celery and onion; bring to a boil. Reduce heat to medium-low; cover and simmer for 20 minutes. In a blender or food processor, process mixture in small batches until smooth. In the same saucepan, cook chopped tomatoes in butter for about 5 minutes; stir in flour. Add half-and-half; cook and stir over low heat until thickened. Stir in processed broth mixture and sugar; heat through without boiling.

A favorite grilled cheese sandwich is delicious in winter
with a steaming bowl of tomato soup. And delicious
in summer paired with produce fresh from the garden!

Triple-Take Grilled Cheese

Makes 4 sandwiches

1 T. oil
8 slices sourdough bread
1/4 c. butter, softened and divided
4 slices American cheese
4 slices Muenster cheese

1/2 c. shredded sharp Cheddar
  cheese
Optional: 4 slices red onion,
  4 slices tomato,
  1/4 c. chopped fresh basil

Heat oil in a skillet over medium heat. Spread 2 bread slices with
one tablespoon butter; place one slice butter-side down on skillet. Layer
one slice American, one slice Muenster and 2 tablespoons Cheddar
cheese on bread. If desired, top with an onion slice, a tomato slice and
one tablespoon basil. Place second buttered bread slice on top of sandwich
in skillet. Reduce heat to medium-low. Cook until golden on one side,
about 3 to 5 minutes; flip and cook until golden on the other side. Repeat
with remaining ingredients.

Add cubes of toasted sourdough or herb
bread to the bottoms of soup bowls and ladle
in steaming soup. Yummy!

Spicy Chili Crackers

Makes 15 to 18 servings

16-oz. pkg. saltine crackers
1 c. olive oil
1-oz. pkg. ranch salad
    dressing mix

2 t. chili seasoning mix
1 t. garlic powder
Optional: cayenne pepper
    to taste

Place crackers in a large bowl; set aside. Combine remaining ingredients in a separate bowl and stir to mix. Pour over crackers; gently stir and let stand overnight. If desired, spread crackers on a baking sheet and bake at 250 degrees for 20 to 30 minutes. Store in an airtight container.

Canned hominy makes a tasty, filling addition to
any southwestern-style soup.

White Chicken Chili

Serves 6 to 8

4 cooked chicken breasts,
    shredded
48-oz. jar Great Northern beans,
    drained
2 c. chicken broth
1 c. salsa

1 T. dried cumin
salt and pepper to taste
2 c. shredded Cheddar cheese
Garnish: shredded Cheddar
    cheese, sour cream,
    saltine crackers

Add all ingredients except cheese and garnish to a 4 to 5-quart slow cooker; stir. Cover and cook on high setting for 5 to 6 hours, or on low setting for 10 to 12 hours. Add cheese in the last one to 2 hours; cover and continue cooking. Garnish as desired.

Turn leftover hot dog buns into garlic bread sticks in a jiffy. Spread buns with softened butter, sprinkle with garlic salt and broil until toasty.

Fred's Chunky Chili

Serves 4 to 6

1 lb. ground beef or turkey,
  browned and drained
3/4 c. onion, diced
3/4 c. green pepper, diced
1 t. garlic, minced
6-oz. can tomato paste
14-1/2 oz. can stewed tomatoes
15-1/2 oz. can kidney beans

1/4 c. salsa
1 T. sugar
1/2 t. cayenne pepper
1/2 t. dried cilantro
1 t. dried basil
Garnish: shredded Cheddar
  cheese, crackers

In a Dutch oven over medium heat, brown beef with onion, green pepper and garlic; drain. Stir in remaining ingredients; do not drain tomatoes or beans. Bring to a simmer over medium-high heat. Cover and simmer over low heat for 30 minutes, stirring occasionally. Serve with cheese and crackers.

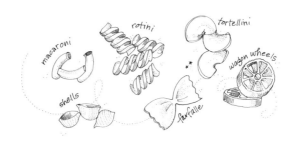

Did you know that you can cook pasta in the slow cooker?
If you're adding dry pasta to a recipe, be sure the sauce
is fairly watery, because the pasta will absorb a lot of
the water as it cooks. Add pasta towards the end of cooking
time and stir well. Serve as soon as pasta reaches desired
tenderness, about 20 to 30 minutes.

Yummy Pizza Soup

Serves 8 to 10

1 lb. ground beef
1 lb. ground Italian pork sausage
1 onion, chopped
8-oz. pkg. sliced pepperoni
28-oz. can crushed tomatoes
2 8-oz. cans tomato sauce
4-1/4 oz. can chopped black
    olives, drained
3 cubes chicken bouillon

2 c. water
1 t. dried oregano
1 t. dried basil
1 t. garlic powder
16-oz. pkg. medium shell
    pasta, uncooked
Garnish: 2 c. shredded mozzarella
    cheese

In a large skillet over medium heat, brown beef, sausage and onion; drain. Add beef mixture to a slow cooker; stir in remaining ingredients except pasta and cheese. Cover and cook on low setting for 4 to 6 hours. About 15 minutes before serving, cook pasta according to package directions; drain. Serve soup ladled over pasta in individual bowls; top with cheese.

If you like your cornbread extra crisp, prepare it
in a vintage sectioned cast-iron skillet. Each wedge
of cornbread will bake up with its own golden crust.

Hasty Tasty Super-Moist Cornbread

Makes 6 to 7 servings

1/3 c. butter, sliced
2 eggs, lightly beaten
8-oz. container sour cream
1 c. canned creamed corn

1 c. self-rising white or
   yellow cornmeal
Optional: hot pepper sauce
   to taste

Add butter to a 9" cast-iron skillet. Set in the oven to melt at 400 degrees for 5 minutes. In a bowl, stir together eggs, sour cream and corn. Whisk in cornmeal and hot sauce, if using, just until combined. Carefully pour batter into hot skillet. Bake at 400 degrees for 30 minutes, or until golden. Cut into wedges to serve.

Stir up a loaf of beer bread to go with White Cheddar-Ale Soup.
Combine 3 cups self-rising flour, a 12-ounce can of beer and
3 tablespoons sugar in a greased loaf pan. Bake for 25 minutes
at 350 degrees, then drizzle with melted butter.

White Cheddar-Ale Soup

Serves 6

2 T. butter
1 onion, diced
2 carrots, peeled and diced
4 cloves garlic, minced
1/3 c. all-purpose flour
1 c. ale or chicken broth
1 T. Worcestershire sauce
2 c. milk

2 c. chicken broth
8-oz. pkg. shredded sharp white
    Cheddar cheese
1/2 to 1 c. shredded Swiss cheese
salt and pepper to taste
Garnish: crushed honey-mustard
    & onion flavored pretzels
Optional: hot pepper sauce

Melt butter in a stockpot over medium heat. Sauté onion and carrots until softened, about 20 minutes. Add garlic to onion mixture; cook an additional minute. Add flour; cook, stirring constantly, for 3 to 4 minutes. Add ale or one cup broth and cook, stirring constantly, for 3 minutes. Stir in Worcestershire sauce, milk and 2 cups broth; simmer for 12 minutes. Purée soup in batches in a food processor. Return soup to pot and turn heat to medium-low. Add cheese, a handful at a time, stirring constantly until cheese has melted. Do not allow soup to boil. Season with salt and pepper. Garnish individual servings with crushed pretzels and hot sauce, if using.

A hearty dish like Spicy Italian Sausage Stew is perfect on a cool autumn night. Carry the stockpot right out to your backyard picnic table and savor the fall colors with your family!

Spicy Italian Sausage Stew

Serves 8

1-1/2 lb. spicy ground Italian
    pork sausage
2 onions, diced
1 green pepper, diced
4 cloves garlic, minced
6 c. chicken broth
28-oz. can diced tomatoes

1 c. ditalini pasta, uncooked
2 sprigs fresh rosemary
6-oz. pkg. fresh baby spinach
2 T. balsamic vinegar
1 t. salt
Garnish: grated Parmesan cheese

Brown sausage in a stockpot over medium heat. Drain on paper towels,
reserving one tablespoon drippings in stockpot. Sauté onions and pepper
in drippings until tender, about 8 minutes. Add garlic and cook an
additional minute. Stir in sausage, broth, tomatoes with juice, uncooked
pasta and rosemary. Bring to a simmer and cook for 10 to 15 minutes,
until pasta is tender. Remove from heat; discard rosemary sprigs. Stir in
spinach, vinegar and salt. Let stand for 2 to 3 minutes, until spinach is
wilted. Top individual servings with cheese.

Quesadillas are quick and filling partners for a bowl
of soup! Sprinkle a flour tortilla with shredded cheese,
top with another tortilla and microwave on high until
the cheese melts. Cut into wedges and serve with salsa.

Unstuffed Green Pepper Soup

Serves 10

1-1/2 lbs. ground turkey
3 green peppers, chopped
1 onion, chopped
2 cloves garlic, minced
2 14-1/2 oz. cans tomato soup

2 14-1/2 oz. cans low-sodium
  beef broth
28-oz. can crushed tomatoes
1-1/2 c. cooked brown rice

In a large stockpot over medium heat, brown turkey with peppers, onion and garlic; drain. Stir in soup, broth and crushed tomatoes with juice; bring to a boil. Reduce heat to low. Cover and simmer until slightly thickened, about 30 minutes. Stir in cooked rice just before serving.

To enjoy the flavor of life, take big bites.

—Robert Heinlein

Italian Beef Dip Sandwiches *Makes 10 to 12 sandwiches*

2 10-1/2 oz. cans beef consommé
    or beef broth
16-oz. jar pepperoncini peppers
0.7-oz. pkg. Italian salad dressing
    mix
1/2 c. water

1 t. salt
4-lb. beef chuck roast
10 to 12 hoagie or ciabatta
    rolls, split
10 to 12 slices provolone cheese

In a Dutch oven, combine consommé or broth, peppers with juice, salad dressing mix, water and salt. Stir to mix well. Add roast; turn to coat. Bake, covered, at 325 degrees for 2-1/2 to 3 hours, until beef is very tender. Shred beef with 2 forks. Spoon some of the beef mixture onto the bottom half of each roll; top with a slice of cheese and top of roll. Bake sandwiches on a baking sheet at 400 degrees for 5 to 8 minutes, until cheese is melted and rolls are crisp. Serve sandwiches with some juice from the Dutch oven for dipping.

Look for different kinds of breads like multi-grain,
sourdough, oatmeal and marble rye...there are
so many choices for tasty sandwiches!

Tailgate Sandwich Ring

2 11-oz. tubes refrigerated
   French bread dough
1/2 lb. bacon, crisply cooked
   and crumbled
3/4 c. mayonnaise
1 T. green onions, chopped

1/2 lb. deli sliced turkey
1/2 lb. deli sliced ham
1/2 lb. sliced provolone cheese
2 tomatoes, sliced
2 c. lettuce, chopped

Spray a Bundt® pan with non-stick vegetable spray. Place both tubes of
dough into pan, seam-side up, joining ends together to form one large
ring. Pinch edges to seal tightly. Lightly spray top of dough with non-
stick vegetable spray. Bake at 350 degrees for 40 to 45 minutes, until
golden. Carefully turn out; cool completely. Combine bacon, mayonnaise
and onions; mix well. Slice bread horizontally. Spread half the bacon
mixture over bottom half of bread. Top with turkey, ham and provolone.
Place on an ungreased baking sheet. Bake at 350 degrees for 5 minutes,
or until cheese melts. Top with tomatoes and lettuce. Spread remaining
bacon mixture on top half of bread; place over lettuce. Slice into wedges.

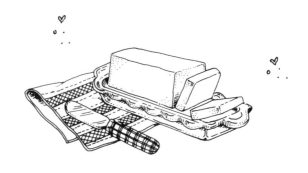

If you're making a sandwich several hours before serving, first spread a light layer of softened butter on the bread. This prevents the bread from absorbing the moisture from the filling and becoming soggy.

Cakewich

1 loaf sliced honey wheat bread
8-oz. pkg. thinly sliced deli turkey
6 slices provolone cheese
1/4 c. mustard
1/2 c. sliced pickles
9-oz. pkg. thinly sliced deli ham
6 slices Swiss cheese

1/4 head lettuce, shredded
3 slices tomato
7-oz. pkg. thinly sliced roast beef
6 slices Pepper Jack cheese
1/4 c. spicy mustard
1/4 c. mayonnaise
Garnish: 10 olives

Press 5 slices of bread in a single layer into the bottom of a 10" round springform pan. Layer turkey, provolone cheese, mustard and pickles on top of bread. Top pickles with another 5 slices of bread. Layer ham, Swiss cheese, lettuce and tomato on top of second bread layer. Press another 5 slices of bread on top of tomatoes. Layer roast beef, Pepper Jack cheese and spicy mustard on top of third bread layer. Top with 5 more bread slices. Release springform pan and remove cake to a serving plate; spread top with mayonnaise to resemble frosting. Garnish with olives, fastened with toothpicks. Cut into slices to serve.

Top bowls of hot soup with plain or cheesy popcorn
instead of croutons for a crunchy surprise.

Creamy Chicken & Gnocchi Soup

Serves 4

1/2 onion, diced
1 stalk celery, diced
1/2 carrot, peeled and shredded
1 clove garlic, diced
1 T. olive oil
3 boneless, skinless chicken
    breasts, cooked and diced
4 c. chicken broth
2 c. half-and-half

1 T. dried thyme
1/8 t. salt
1/8 t. pepper
16-oz. pkg. gnocchi pasta,
    uncooked
1/2 c. fresh spinach, chopped
1 T. cornstarch
2 T. cold water

In a large soup pot over medium heat, sauté onion, celery, carrot and garlic in oil until onion is translucent. Stir in chicken, chicken broth, half-and-half and seasonings; bring to a boil. Add uncooked gnocchi; cook for 4 minutes. Reduce heat to medium-low. Continue cooking for 10 minutes, stirring often. Add spinach; cook for one to 2 minutes, until spinach is wilted. In a cup, dissolve cornstarch in cold water. Return soup to boiling; add cornstarch mixture. Cook and stir until thickened.

Serve steaming chowder in hollowed-out rounds of sourdough bread. To make yummy croutons, cut the scooped-out bread into one-inch cubes. Season to your liking; lightly toast in an oiled, hot skillet.

Manhattan Clam Chowder

Serves 4 to 6

1/2 lb. bacon, chopped
1 onion, sliced
2 cloves garlic, minced
28-oz. can whole tomatoes
2 6-1/2 oz. cans minced clams
8-oz. bottle clam juice

1 T. dried thyme
salt and pepper to taste
10-oz. pkg. frozen soup
  vegetables
1 to 2 potatoes, peeled and diced

Add bacon, onion and garlic to a skillet over medium heat; cook and stir until bacon is crisp and onion is tender. Drain; add to a slow cooker. Add undrained tomatoes, undrained clams, clam juice and seasonings. Cover and cook on high setting for 2 hours. Add vegetables and potatoes. Cover; reduce heat to low and cook for 3 to 4 hours longer, until vegetables are tender.

When cooking seafood in the slow cooker, add it
during the last hour of cooking time, or it may
overcook and have a rubbery texture.

Savory Shrimp Bisque

Serves 4 to 6

2 10-3/4 oz. cans cream of
    potato soup
10-3/4 oz. can of mushroom soup
8-oz. pkg. cream cheese, cubed
15-1/4 oz. can corn, drained

1 to 2 T. Cajun seasoning
1 lb. frozen small shrimp, thawed
1 bunch green onions, chopped
1/2 c. margarine
1 qt. half-and-half

Mix soups, cream cheese, corn and seasoning in a slow cooker. Cover and cook on high setting for one to 2 hours, until heated through. In a skillet over medium heat, sauté shrimp and onions in margarine until shrimp are pink. Add shrimp mixture to slow cooker; stir in half-and-half. Cover and cook on low setting for one hour longer.

Stir up a scrumptious dill sauce for salmon or tuna patties.
Blend 1/2 cup sour cream, one tablespoon Dijon mustard,
one tablespoon lemon juice and 2 teaspoons chopped
fresh dill. Chill before serving.

Grilled Salmon BLTs

1/3 c. mayonnaise
2 t. fresh dill, chopped
1 t. lemon zest
4 salmon fillets, 1-inch thick
1/4 t. salt
1/8 t. pepper

8 slices country-style bread,
   1/2-inch thick
4 romaine lettuce leaves
2 tomatoes, sliced
6 slices bacon, crisply cooked
   and halved

Stir together mayonnaise, dill and zest in a small bowl; set aside. Sprinkle salmon with salt and pepper; place on a lightly greased hot grill, skin-side down. Cover and cook over medium heat about 10 to 12 minutes, without turning, until cooked through. Slide a thin metal spatula between salmon and skin; lift salmon and transfer to a plate. Discard skin. Arrange bread slices on grill; cook until lightly toasted on both sides. Spread mayonnaise mixture on one side of 4 bread slices. Top each bread slice with one lettuce leaf, 2 tomato slices, 3 half-slices bacon, one salmon fillet and remaining bread slice.

Use mini cookie cutters to make whimsical soup croutons...
kids will love them! Cut out fun shapes from slices of
day-old bread, brush with butter and bake at
200 degrees until croutons are crunchy and golden.

Quick Cheese Biscuits

Makes 1-1/2 dozen

2 c. biscuit baking mix
2/3 c. milk
2/3 c. shredded Cheddar cheese

1/4 c. butter, melted
1 t. garlic powder

In a bowl, combine baking mix, milk and cheese; mix well. Drop batter by heaping tablespoonfuls onto a lightly greased baking sheet. Bake at 450 degrees for 8 to 10 minutes. Combine butter and garlic powder; brush over hot biscuits when they come out of the oven.

For the most flavorful chicken soup, use bone-in,
skin-on chicken. Skin and bones are easily removed
after the chicken is cooked. Chill the soup
overnight and skim off the fat before
rewarming and serving your delicious soup.

Creamy Chicken Noodle Soup   *Makes 10 to 12 servings*

8 c. water
8 cubes chicken bouillon
6-1/2 c. wide egg noodles,
    uncooked
2 10-3/4 oz. cans cream of
    chicken soup

3 c. cooked chicken, cubed
8-oz. container sour cream
Optional: shredded Cheddar
    cheese, chopped fresh parsley

In a large saucepan over high heat, bring water and bouillon to a boil; stir until bouillon dissolves. Add noodles and cook until tender, about 10 minutes. Do not drain. Reduce heat to medium. Stir in soup and chicken; heat through. Remove from heat; stir in sour cream. If desired, top servings with cheese and parsley.

A pretty cut-glass biscuit jar isn't just for holding cookies or crackers...fill it with crisp bread sticks or pretzel rods to serve with soup.

Fluffy Chicken & Dumplings

Serves 6

1 to 2 T. oil
1 c. celery, chopped
1 c. carrots, peeled and sliced
1 T. onion, chopped
49-oz. can chicken broth
10-3/4 oz. can cream of
   chicken soup

1/8 t. pepper
2 c. cooked chicken, chopped
1-2/3 c. biscuit baking mix
2/3 c. milk
Garnish: chopped fresh parsley

Heat oil in a Dutch oven over medium-high heat; sauté celery, carrots and onion for 7 minutes, or until crisp-tender. Add broth, soup and pepper; bring to a boil. Reduce heat to low; stir in chicken and continue to simmer. To make dumplings, stir together baking mix and milk in a bowl. Drop by large spoonfuls into simmering broth. Cover and cook over low heat for 15 minutes without lifting the lid, to allow dumplings to cook. Garnish with parsley.

For a party or potluck, roll up sets of flatware in table napkins and place in a shallow tray. An easy do-ahead for the hostess... guests will find it simple to pull out individual sets too.

Shredded Chicken Sandwiches

Makes 8 servings

1/4 c. olive oil
4 boneless, skinless chicken
  breasts
1 onion, chopped
10-3/4 oz. can cream of
  mushroom soup
1 c. chicken broth

1/2 c. sherry or chicken broth
2 t. soy sauce
2 t. Worcestershire sauce
salt and pepper to taste
8 sandwich buns, split
Optional: pickle slices,
  lettuce leaves

Heat oil in a skillet over medium-high heat; add chicken. Cook for
5 minutes on each side, until golden. Transfer chicken to a slow cooker;
set aside. Add onion to drippings in skillet. Sauté until golden; drain.
Add soup, broth, sherry or broth, sauces and seasonings to skillet. Stir
mixture well and spoon over chicken in slow cooker. Cover and cook on
low setting for 6 to 8 hours. Shred chicken with a fork; spoon onto buns.
Garnish with pickles and lettuce, if desired.

An old-fashioned food grinder is handy for grinding meat
for spreads, meatloaf and other recipes. To clean it
easily when you've finished, just put a half-slice of
bread through the grinder. The bread will remove
any food particles.

Pork Sandwich Spread

Makes 20 sandwiches

2 to 3-lb. pork roast
1/4 t. dried basil
1/4 t. dried oregano
salt and pepper to taste
3 eggs, beaten
1 sleeve round buttery crackers,
  crushed

4-oz. jar chopped pimentos,
  drained
1 green pepper, chopped
20 sandwich buns, split
  and warmed

Place roast in a slow cooker; sprinkle with seasonings. Cover and cook on high setting for 2 to 3 hours, until fork-tender. Remove roast to a plate; cool. Reserve 1/2 cup cooking liquid. Grind roast with a meat grinder; transfer to a bowl. Add remaining ingredients except buns, reserved liquid and enough water to obtain the consistency of thick soup. Return mixture to slow cooker and cook on low setting for an additional 2 hours. Spoon pork mixture onto buns.

Warm sandwich buns for a crowd...easy! Fill a roaster
with buns, cover with heavy-duty aluminum foil and cut
several slits in the foil. Top with several dampened paper
towels and tightly cover with more foil. Place in a 250-degree
oven for 20 minutes. Rolls will be hot and steamy.

Shredded Buffalo Chicken Sandwiches

Makes 8 to 12 sandwiches

2-1/2 to 3-lbs. boneless, skinless
    chicken breasts
3-oz. pkg. cream cheese, softened
1 c. buffalo chicken wing sauce

1-oz. pkg. ranch salad
    dressing mix
8 to 12 sandwich buns, split

Arrange chicken in a 5-quart slow cooker; do not add anything. Cover and cook on high setting for 4 hours, or until chicken is no longer pink inside. Use 2 forks to shred chicken in slow cooker. Stir in cream cheese, sauce and salad dressing mix. If mixture is too juicy, cook, uncovered, on low setting for 30 more minutes. Serve chicken mixture on buns.

Ladle individual portions of leftover soup into small
freezer bags...seal, label and freeze. Then, when you
need a quick-fix lunch or dinner, simply transfer soup
to a microwave-safe bowl and reheat.

Country Minestrone

3 slices bacon, diced
1 c. onion, chopped
1/2 c. celery, sliced
14-1/2 oz. can beef broth
10-3/4 oz. can bean with bacon
    soup
1-3/4 to 2 c. water
14-1/2 oz. can diced tomatoes
1 t. dried basil

1/2 t. salt
1/2 t. pepper
8-oz. pkg. elbow macaroni,
    uncooked
1 c. cabbage, chopped
1 c. zucchini, cubed
1 c. yellow squash, cubed
1/2 t. beef bouillon granules

In a skillet over medium-high heat, cook bacon until crisp. Use a slotted spoon to remove bacon and set aside to drain, reserving drippings. In the same skillet, sauté onion and celery in drippings until tender. Stir in broth, soup, water, tomatoes with juice and seasonings. Bring to a boil; reduce heat to medium-low and simmer for 10 minutes. Add remaining ingredients except reserved bacon. Simmer for 10 minutes, or until macaroni and vegetables are tender. Stir in bacon.

Bread bowls make a hearty soup extra special. Cut the tops off round bread loaves and hollow out, then rub with olive oil and garlic. Pop in the oven at 400 degrees for 10 minutes, or until crusty and golden. Ladle in soup and serve right away.

Hungarian Mushroom Soup   *Makes 8 to 10 servings*

1/4 c. onion, diced
8 c. sliced mushrooms
1 c. butter
1 c. all-purpose flour
2 16-oz. cans chicken broth
3 T. paprika

1/4 c. soy sauce
16-oz. container sour cream
1 T. dried parsley
1 T. dill weed
2 T. lemon juice
12-oz. can evaporated milk

In a stockpot over medium heat, sauté onion and mushrooms in butter, until tender. Stir in flour. Add remaining ingredients except evaporated milk; bring to a simmer. Stir in milk. Cover and simmer over low heat for about one hour, stirring occasionally.

Just for fun, serve up soft pretzels instead of dinner rolls...
so easy, the kids can do it! Twist strips of refrigerated
bread stick dough into pretzel shapes and place on an
ungreased baking sheet. Brush with beaten egg white,
sprinkle with coarse salt and bake as the package directs.

Ham & Potato Soup

Makes 8 servings

3-1/2 c. potatoes, peeled
    and diced
1/3 c. celery, chopped
1/3 c. onion, finely chopped
3/4 c. cooked ham, diced
3-1/4 c. water

6 cubes chicken bouillon
1/2 t. salt
1 t. pepper
5 T. butter
5 T. all-purpose flour
2 c. milk

In a slow cooker, combine all ingredients except butter, flour and milk. Cover and cook on low setting for 6 to 8 hours, until potatoes are fork-tender. About 20 minutes before serving, melt butter in a saucepan over medium heat; stir in flour. Gradually add milk, stirring constantly until thickened. Stir mixture into soup in slow cooker. Cover and cook on low setting an additional 15 to 20 minutes, until thickened.

Sandwiches are a tasty solution when family members will be dining at different times. Fix sandwiches ahead of time, wrap individually and refrigerate. Pop them into a toaster oven or under a broiler to heat...fresh, full of flavor and ready whenever you are!

Pocket Sammies

Makes 12 sandwiches

1 lb. ground beef
1/2 c. onion, diced
1 c. barbecue sauce

12 frozen dinner rolls, thawed
12 slices American cheese

In a skillet over medium heat, brown beef and onion; drain. Add barbecue sauce to beef mixture; simmer until thickened, about 5 minutes. Roll out each roll into a 6-inch round. Evenly divide beef mixture among dough rounds; top each with a slice of cheese. Fold over edges and crimp seams together with a fork. Place on a lightly greased baking sheet. Bake at 400 degrees for 15 minutes, or until golden.

Store unwashed, dry mushrooms in the refrigerator.
The mushrooms will stay fresher longer if they're
placed in a paper bag rather than a plastic bag.

Mushroom & Steak Hoagies

Serves 6

1 c. water
1/3 c. soy sauce
1-1/2 t. garlic powder
1-1/2 t. pepper
1-lb. beef round steak, cut into
    1/4-inch strips
1 to 2 T. oil

1 onion, sliced
1 green pepper, thinly sliced
4-oz. can mushroom stems &
    pieces, drained
2 c. shredded mozzarella cheese
6 hoagie buns, split

Whisk together water, soy sauce, garlic powder and pepper in a bowl.
Add steak, turning to coat. Cover and refrigerate overnight. Drain and
discard marinade; brown steak in oil in a large skillet over medium-high
heat. Add onion, green pepper and mushrooms; sauté for 8 minutes, or
until tender. Reduce heat; top with cheese. Remove from heat; stir until
cheese melts and steak is coated. Spoon onto buns to serve.

Saucy sandwiches are best served on a vintage-style
oilcloth...spills wipe right up! Look for one with a
colorful design of fruit, flowers or even in
your favorite team's colors.

Slow-Cooker Cheesesteak Sandwiches

Makes 4 sandwiches

1 lb. beef round steak,
   thinly sliced
1/2 onion, diced
1 red pepper, diced
1-1/2 t. garlic powder
1 T. butter

1 T. Worcestershire sauce
1 cube beef bouillon
16-oz. pkg. shredded Colby
   Jack cheese
4 hoagie rolls, split

Add all ingredients except cheese and rolls to a lightly greased slow cooker. Pour in enough water to just cover the ingredients. Cover and cook on low setting for 6 to 8 hours. Using a slotted spoon, place a serving of steak mixture on the bottom of each roll; sprinkle with cheese. Replace tops of rolls to make sandwiches.

Keep a few quart-size Mason jars tucked in the cupboard
so you can send home some homemade soup with a
dinner guest...what a thoughtful gesture!

Cider Mill Stew

Makes 4 servings

3 T. all-purpose flour
1 t. salt
1/2 t. pepper
1 lb. stew beef cubes
2 T. oil
1 c. apple cider
1 c. water
1 c. beef broth

1 T. cider vinegar
1/2 t. dried thyme
2 carrots, peeled and cut into
    1-inch pieces
1 stalk celery, cut into
    1-inch pieces
1 potato, peeled and cubed
1 onion, sliced

Combine flour, salt and pepper in a large plastic zipping bag. Add beef, a few pieces at a time; shake to coat. In a Dutch oven over medium heat, brown beef in oil; drain. Stir in cider, water, broth, vinegar and thyme; bring to a boil over medium heat. Reduce heat to medium-low; cover and simmer for one hour and 45 minutes, or until beef is tender. Add vegetables; return to a boil. Reduce heat; cover and simmer for 30 minutes, or until vegetables are tender.

Oops! If a soup or stew begins to burn on the bottom, all is not lost. Spoon it into another pan, being careful not to scrape up the scorched food on the bottom. The burnt taste usually won't linger.

6-Pack Texas Stew

Serves 6 to 8

1-1/2 lbs. stew beef cubes
1/3 c. bacon, finely chopped
1 onion, chopped
3 T. paprika
1 T. salt
1 t. dried marjoram
2 12-oz. cans regular or
    non-alcoholic beer

1 c. water
8-oz. can tomato sauce
1 T. Worcestershire sauce
4 potatoes, peeled and cubed
1-1/2 c. baby carrots, sliced
1-1/2 c. turnips, peeled and sliced

Brown beef and bacon in a large stockpot over medium heat. Remove beef and bacon to a bowl, reserving one tablespoon drippings in stockpot. Add onion to drippings and cook until translucent. Return beef and bacon to stockpot and add seasonings, beer, water and sauces; stir to combine. Reduce heat to low; cover and simmer until beef is very tender, about 1-1/2 hours. Add vegetables; cover and simmer until tender, about 45 additional minutes.

Keep fresh-baked bread warm and toasty! Slip a piece of aluminum foil into the bread basket, then top it with a decorative napkin.

Best-Ever Garlic Bread

Makes one loaf

3/4 c. butter, softened
6 T. mayonnaise
3/4 c. grated Parmesan cheese
2 T. fresh parsley, chopped

3 cloves garlic, minced
1/2 t. dried oregano
1 loaf French bread, halved
  lengthwise

In a small bowl, blend together all ingredients except bread. Spread butter mixture over cut sides of bread. Wrap bread halves in 2 pieces of aluminum foil; place cut-side up on a baking sheet. Bake at 375 degrees for 20 minutes. Unwrap bread and discard foil; place bread on a broiler pan. Broil until golden, about 2 minutes. Slice and serve warm.

Prewarmed soup bowls are a thoughtful touch.
Set oven-safe crocks on a baking sheet and tuck into
a warm oven for a few minutes. Ladle in hot,
hearty soup...mmm, pass the cornbread!

Split Pea Soup with Ham

Makes 6 servings

2 c. cooked ham, cubed
1 c. dried split peas
1 c. onion, chopped
1 c. celery with leaves, chopped
1 c. carrot, peeled and shredded

1/2 t. dried thyme
1/4 t. pepper
1 bay leaf
4 c. chicken broth
2 c. water

Combine ham, dried peas, vegetables and seasonings in a 4-quart slow cooker. Pour broth and water over all; stir. Cover and cook on low setting for 10 to 12 hours, or on high setting for 4 to 5 hours. Discard bay leaf before serving.

Do you have a big pot of leftover soup? Be sure to transfer the extra soup into smaller containers before refrigerating or freezing. The soup will reach a safe temperature much more quickly.

Spicy Pork & Sweet Potato Chili *Makes 6 to 8 servings*

1 T. oil
1 onion, chopped
1 sweet potato, peeled and cut
    into 1/2-inch cubes
3 cloves garlic, chopped
15-1/2 oz. can diced tomatoes
4 c. chicken broth

15-1/2 oz. can white beans,
    drained
12-oz. jar tomatillo green salsa
2 T. chili powder
1 bay leaf
1 lb. cooked pork roast, cut into
    1/2-inch cubes

Heat oil in a Dutch oven over medium heat. Add onion, sweet potato and garlic; sauté about 7 minutes. Stir in tomatoes with juice and remaining ingredients except pork cubes. Reduce heat to medium-low and simmer for about 30 minutes, stirring occasionally. Stir in pork cubes; simmer for 5 minutes. Discard bay leaf before serving.

Do you have a favorite soup recipe that you don't serve often due to lack of time? Try making it in a slow cooker instead! A recipe that simmers for 2 hours on the stovetop can generally cook all day on the low setting without overcooking.

Chicken Enchilada Soup

1 onion, chopped
1 clove garlic, pressed
1 to 2 t. oil
14-1/2 oz. can beef broth
14-1/2 oz. can chicken broth
10-3/4 oz. can cream of
   chicken soup
1-1/2 c. water
12-1/2 oz. can chicken, drained

4-oz. can chopped green chiles
2 t. Worcestershire sauce
1 T. steak sauce
1 t. ground cumin
1 t. chili powder
1/8 t. pepper
6 corn tortillas, cut into strips
1 c. shredded Cheddar cheese

In a stockpot over medium heat, sauté onion and garlic in oil. Add remaining ingredients except tortilla strips and cheese; bring to a boil. Cover; reduce heat and simmer for one hour, stirring occasionally. Uncover; stir in tortilla strips and cheese. Simmer an additional 10 minutes.

"Fried" ice cream is a fun & festive ending to a Mexican meal.
Roll scoops of ice cream in a mixture of crushed frosted
corn flake cereal and cinnamon. Garnish with a drizzle of honey
and a dollop of whipped topping. They'll ask for seconds!

Chicken Quesadillas El Grande

Serves 8

1 lb. sliced roast deli chicken, shredded
3 T. salsa
salt and pepper to taste
1/2 c. onion, cut into strips
1 green pepper, cut into strips
3 T. olive oil

15-oz. can refried beans
8 10-inch flour tortillas
6-oz. pkg. shredded Mexican-blend cheese
Garnish: shredded lettuce, diced tomatoes, sour cream, diced onion, additional salsa

In a bowl, stir together chicken, salsa, salt and pepper; set aside. In a skillet over medium heat, cook onion and pepper in oil until crisp-tender; remove to a bowl. Evenly spread refried beans onto 4 tortillas. For each quesadilla, place one tortilla, bean-side up, in a skillet coated with non-stick vegetable spray. Top with 1/4 each of chicken, onion mixture and cheese; place a plain tortilla on top. Cook over medium heat until layers start to warm, about 2 minutes. Flip over and cook until tortilla is crisp and filling is hot. Cut each quesadilla into wedges and garnish as desired.

When burgers and hot dogs are on the menu, set out
a muffin tin filled with shredded cheese, catsup or salsa,
crispy bacon and other yummy stuff. Everyone can
just help themselves to their favorite toppings.

Mexican Burgers

Makes 5 sandwiches

1 avocado, peeled, pitted
    and diced
1 plum tomato, diced
2 green onions, chopped
1 to 2 t. lime juice
1-1/4 lbs. ground beef
1 egg, beaten
3/4 c. to 1 c. nacho-flavored
    tortilla chips, crushed

1/4 c. fresh cilantro, chopped
1/2 t. chili powder
1/2 t. ground cumin
salt and pepper to taste
1-1/4 c. shredded Pepper
    Jack cheese
5 hamburger buns, split

Combine avocado, tomato, onions and lime juice; mash slightly and set aside. Combine beef, egg, chips and seasonings in a large bowl. Mix well and form into 5 patties. Grill over medium-high heat to desired doneness, turning to cook on both sides. Sprinkle cheese over burgers; grill until melted. Place burgers on bottoms of buns; top with avocado mixture and bun tops.

Soups are ideal for casual tailgating get-togethers.
Borrow three or four slow cookers and fill each
with a different soup, stew or chowder. Or, better yet,
ask friends to bring their favorite soup to share!

The Best Chicken & Corn Chowder

Makes 4 to 6 servings

3 T. butter
4 boneless, skinless chicken
    breasts, cooked and shredded
1/2 c. onion, chopped
2 cloves garlic
2 cubes chicken bouillon

1 c. hot water
2 c. half-and-half
2 c. shredded Monterey
    Jack cheese
14-3/4 oz. can creamed corn
4-oz. can chopped green chiles

Melt butter in a large Dutch oven over medium heat. Cook chicken, onion and garlic in butter until chicken is heated through and onion is translucent, about 10 minutes. Meanwhile, dissolve bouillon cubes in hot water. Pour bouillon mixture into chicken mixture; bring to a boil. Reduce heat to medium-low; add remaining ingredients. Stir until cheese is completely melted.

Not enough soup bowls on hand for family & friends?
Open the cupboards and pull out sturdy mugs!
They're just as nice, and the handles make them
easy to hold.

Bacon-Cheeseburger Soup

Serves 8 to 12

1-1/2 lbs. ground beef or turkey,
    or a combination
salt and pepper to taste
3-oz. pkg real bacon bits
32-oz. container chicken broth

32-oz. pkg. pasteurized process
    cheese, sliced and quartered
24-oz. pkg. frozen southern-style
    diced hashbrown potatoes

Brown beef or turkey in a large skillet over medium heat; drain. Season
with salt and pepper; transfer to a 6-quart slow cooker. Add remaining
ingredients; stir well. Cover and cook on low setting for 6 to 8 hours,
until hot and cheese is melted, stirring occasionally.

The ultimate comfort food...place a scoop of
mashed potatoes in the center of a soup bowl,
then ladle hearty soup all around the potatoes.

Creamy Turkey-Vegetable Soup *Makes 8 to 10 servings*

1 onion, finely chopped
2 T. butter
3 c. new redskin potatoes, diced
2 14-1/2 oz. cans chicken broth
2 c. cooked turkey, cubed

2 c. frozen mixed vegetables, thawed
1/2 t. white pepper
1/2 t. poultry seasoning
2 c. whipping cream

In a soup pot over medium heat, sauté onion in butter until tender. Add potatoes and broth; bring to a boil. Reduce heat to medium-low; cover and simmer for 20 minutes. Stir in turkey, vegetables and seasonings. Simmer another 10 to 12 minutes, until vegetables are tender. Stir in cream; heat through without boiling.

A tasty apple coleslaw goes well with most any burger or sandwich. Simply toss together a large bag of coleslaw mix and a chopped Granny Smith apple. Stir in coleslaw dressing to desired consistency.

Bestest Burger Ever

2 lbs. lean ground beef
1 onion, chopped
1 t. salt
1 t. pepper
1 t. dried basil
1/3 c. teriyaki sauce
1/4 c. Italian-seasoned dry
    bread crumbs

1 T. grated Parmesan cheese
4 slices American cheese, halved
8 sesame wheat rolls, split
Garnish: fresh arugula, sliced
    cucumber

Mix together beef, onion, salt, pepper and basil. Add teriyaki sauce,
bread crumbs and Parmesan cheese; mix well and divide into 8 patties.
Grill to desired doneness; top with American cheese. Serve on rolls,
garnished as desired.

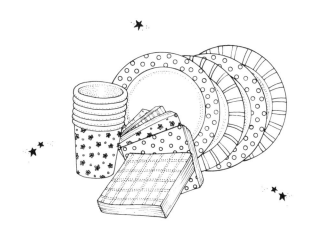

Declare a Picnic Night at home! Just toss a checkered
tablecloth on the dinner table and set out paper plates
and disposable plastic utensils. Relax and enjoy dinner...
no dishes to wash!

Root Beer Pulled Pork Sandwiches

Makes 6 to 8 servings

3-lb. pork butt roast, or
   2 pork tenderloins
12-oz. bottle root beer
18-oz. bottle favorite
   barbecue sauce

6 to 8 hamburger buns, split
   and toasted
Garnish: coleslaw

Place roast in a slow cooker; pour root beer over it. Cover and cook on low setting for 6 to 8 hours, until easily shredded with a fork. Remove roast from cooker; discard juices. Shred roast and return to slow cooker. Pour barbecue sauce over pork. Cover and cook on low setting about 30 minutes, until heated through. Serve pork on toasted buns, topped with coleslaw.

Cloth napkins make mealtime just a little more special...
and they're a must when serving soup! Stitch or
hot-glue fun charms to napkin rings, so family
members can identify their own napkin easily.

French Onion Soup

Makes 6 servings

6 onions, thinly sliced
1 T. oil
4 T. butter, divided
6 c. beef broth
salt and pepper to taste
1/2 c. Gruyère cheese,
    shredded and divided

1/2 c. shredded Swiss cheese,
    divided
1/2 c. grated Parmesan cheese,
    divided
6 slices French bread, toasted

Cook onions in oil and 2 tablespoons butter over low heat in a 3-quart saucepan until tender; add broth. Bring to a boil; reduce heat and simmer for 30 minutes. Remove from heat; season with salt and pepper. Ladle equally into 6 oven-safe serving bowls; sprinkle each bowl with equal amounts of each cheese. Arrange one bread slice on top of cheeses. Melt remaining butter; drizzle over bread slices. Place bowls on a baking sheet; bake at 425 degrees for 10 minutes. Broil until cheeses are golden; serve immediately.

Okra helps thicken soups and stews...it's tasty too!
When cut, the raw okra releases a syrupy liquid that
thickens broths while it cooks.

South Carolina Gumbo

Serves 4 to 6

1 T. olive oil
1 onion, chopped
1 stalk celery, sliced
1/2 green pepper, chopped
2 c. boneless, skinless chicken
    breasts, cubed
2 c. okra, chopped
2 14-1/2 oz. cans chicken broth

1 c. water
14-1/2 oz. can diced tomatoes,
    drained
2 t. Cajun seasoning
1/2 t. garlic powder
1 t. salt
1/2 t. pepper
1 c. instant rice, uncooked

Heat oil in a large stockpot over medium heat. Add onion, celery and green pepper to oil; sauté until tender, about 8 to 10 minutes. Add chicken and remaining ingredients except rice; bring to a boil. Reduce heat to medium-low and simmer, covered, for 15 minutes, or until chicken is fully cooked. Add uncooked rice and simmer 15 more minutes, or until rice is tender.

A fruity cream cheese spread tastes scrumptious on sandwiches.
Just combine one 8-ounce package of softened cream cheese
with 1/4 cup apricot preserves. Stir until smooth. So delicious
on turkey or ham sandwiches!

Blue Cheese Cut-Out Crackers *Makes 1-1/2 to 2 dozen*

1 c. all-purpose flour
7 T. butter, softened
7 T. crumbled blue cheese
1/2 t. dried parsley

1 egg yolk
1/8 t. salt
4 t. whipping cream
cayenne pepper to taste

In a bowl, mix all ingredients together; let rest for 30 minutes. On a lightly floured surface, roll out dough to about 1/8-inch thick. Use small cookie cutters to cut out crackers. Bake on ungreased baking sheets at 400 degrees for 8 to 10 minutes, just until golden. Let cool; remove carefully. Store in an airtight container.

Toad in a Hole, Egg in a Nest...whatever the name, kids love 'em
and they're so easy to fix. Cut out the center of a slice
of bread with a small cookie cutter. Add the bread to
a buttered skillet over medium heat and break an egg into
the hole. Cook until golden on the bottom, turn over with
a spatula and cook until the egg is set as you like.

Ham, Egg & Cheesewich

Makes one serving

2 slices bread, toasted
3 t. butter, softened and divided
1 egg
1 slice American cheese
salt to taste
3 to 4 thin slices cooked deli ham

Spread each slice of toast with one teaspoon butter; set aside. Melt remaining butter in a skillet over medium-low heat. Crack egg into skillet; break yolk with a fork or leave whole. Cook until egg is nearly set; turn over with a spatula. Season with salt; top with cheese and remove to a plate. Add stacked ham to skillet; warm on both sides. Top ham with egg and cheese; sandwich ham and egg stack between toast slices.

Egg sandwiches make a super-quick and tasty meal.
Scramble eggs as you like, tossing in chopped ham or
shredded cheese for extra flavor. Serve on toasted,
buttered English muffins alongside fresh fruit cups...
ready in a flash!

Sausage Muffins

Makes 6 sandwiches

1 lb. ground turkey sausage
1/4 c. butter, sliced
5-oz. jar sharp pasteurized
    process cheese spread

1/4 t. garlic powder
6 English muffins, split

Brown sausage in a skillet over medium heat; drain. Add butter, cheese and garlic powder; cook and stir until cheese melts. Spread sausage mixture on 6 English muffin halves. Place on an ungreased baking sheet. Bake at 350 degrees for 15 minutes, or until heated through. Top with remaining halves of English muffins.

INDEX

INDEX

SOUPS

Our Story

Back in 1984, we were next-door neighbors raising our families in the little town of Delaware, Ohio. Two moms with small children, we were looking for a way to do what we loved and stay home with the kids too. We had always shared a love of home cooking and making memories with family & friends and so, after many a conversation over the backyard fence, **Gooseberry Patch** was born.

We put together our first catalog at our kitchen tables, enlisting the help of our loved ones wherever we could. From that very first mailing, we found an immediate connection with many of our customers and it wasn't long before we began receiving letters, photos and recipes from these new friends. In 1992, we put together our very first cookbook, compiled from hundreds of these recipes and, the rest, as they say, is history.

Hard to believe it's been 40 years since those kitchen-table days! From that original little **Gooseberry Patch** family, we've grown to include an amazing group of creative folks who love cooking, decorating and creating as much as we do. Today, we're best known for our homestyle, family-friendly cookbooks, now recognized as national bestsellers.

One thing's for sure, we couldn't have done it without our friends all across the country. Each year, we're honored to turn thousands of your recipes into our collectible cookbooks. Our hope is that each book captures the stories and heart of all of you who have shared with us. Whether you've been with us since the beginning or are just discovering us, welcome to the **Gooseberry Patch** family!

Jo Ann & Vickie

Visit our website anytime
www.gooseberrypatch.com

Email

1·800·854·6673